Jokes for Kids 10 Books in 1 Awesome Collection

Limited Edition with Bonus Book

I.P. Grinning
&
I.P. Factly

Copyright © 2015 IP Factly

All rights reserved.

ISBN: 1517323525
ISBN-13: 9781517323523

To Jacob, Riley & Having Fun.

Contents:

Jokes for Kids by IP Grinning

Table of Contents

101 Alien Jokes

101 Monster Jokes

101 Dinosaur Jokes

101 Wild Animal Jokes

101 Creepy Crawly Jokes

101 Dog & Cat Jokes

101 Bird Jokes

101 Fish Jokes

101 Farmyard Jokes

101 School Jokes

BONUS BOOK -- 101 Knock Knock Jokes for Kids

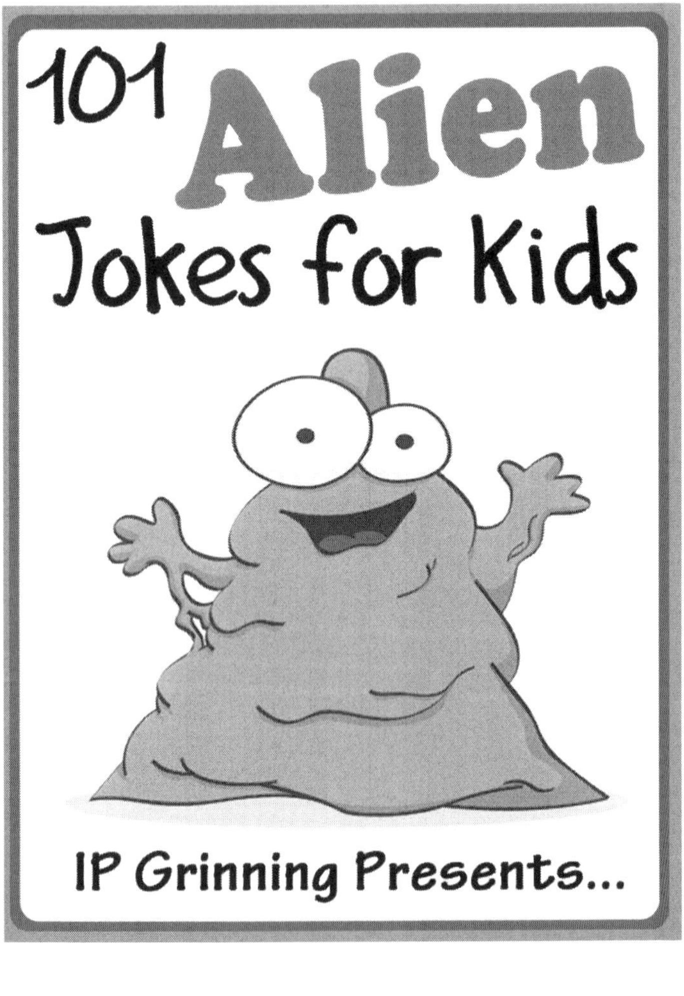
101
Alien
Jokes for Kids
IP Grinning Presents...

1.

What do you say when you greet an alien with four heads?

Hello, hello, hello, hello!

2.

Why was the alien green?

It hadn't taken its space sickness pills!

3.

Which planet in the solar system did the alien crash land on?

Splaturn!

4.
What happened when Ray discovered an alien with a laser gun?

He became an ex-Ray!

5.
Where should a 500 pound alien go?

On a diet!

6.
What is a space alien's favorite thing to have on toast?

Baked beings!

7.

What's the best way to talk to aliens?

From a long way away!

8.

What would you get if you crossed a UFO with a wizard?

A flying sorcerer!

9.

How would throwing eggs at aliens destroy them?

They'd be eggs-terminated!

10.

What steps should you take if you see an alien?

Large ones!

11.

What is an alien's favorite soup?

Scream of tomato!

12.

What's the difference between an alien and a cookie?

Have you ever tried dunking an alien in your milk?

13.

What's the difference between an alien and potatoes?

You should never try mashing an alien!

14.

What's got four tentacles, a huge head and wants you to shock it?

An alien with hiccups!

15.

Why are aliens forgetful?

Everything goes in one ear and out the others!

16.

What is the difference between an invading alien fleet and a candy bar?

People like candy!

17.
What can aliens do that humans can't?

Count to 50 on their fingers!

18.
What else can aliens do that humans can't?

Count to 100 on their toes!

19.

When do aliens eat fluorescent lamps?

Whenever they need light refreshments!

20.

Why did the alien cross the road?

It wanted to learn more about the lives of chickens!

21.

What do you give an alien with six huge feet?

Three pairs of flippers!

22.

How do you get ten aliens in a pickle jar?

Eat the pickles first!

23.

What happened when the police tried to find an alien with one eye?

They had more luck when they started using both eyes!

24.

Why did the space alien become known as Captain Kirk?

It had a left ear, a right ear and a final front ear!

25.

Where do the scariest of all space aliens live?

In a far distant terror-tory!

26.

What happened when the boy announced he could lift an alien with both hands tied?

They couldn't find an alien that was tied up!

27.

Why do barbers never cut the hair of aliens with ray guns?

It's easier with scissors!

28.

What happens if you upset a man-eating alien?

You end up in hot water!

29.

What did Jupiter say to Saturn at the end of the phone call?

Give me a ring!

30.

What are the planet's favorite songs?

Nep-tunes!

31.
How do cows move about the galaxy?

Through the Milky Way!

32.
What happened to the man who crossed a toad with the sun?

He got star warts!

33.
Where did the aliens leave their UFOs?

At parking meteors!

34.
What game do aliens play?

Astronauts and crosses!

35.
What was Captain Kirk doing when he went into the ladies bathroom?

Boldly going where no man has been before!

36.
When do astronauts eat?

At launch time!

37.
What are crazy spacemen called?

Astronuts!

38.
What do alien's love to play at parties?

Hide-and-go-shriek!

39.
What's the best thing to become if you've got high hopes?

A spaceman!

40.

What did the super-fast alien say?

Take me to your speeder!

41.

What did the hungry alien say?

Take me to your feeder!

42.

What did the alien that wanted a bedtime story say?

Take me to your reader!

43.

What did the alien say to the messy garden?

Take me to your weeder!

44.

How do aliens shave in the morning?

With a laser blade!

45.

What robot knows the quickest way to any star system?

R2 detour!

46.

Do robots have brothers?

No, but they do have tran-sisters!

47.

How can you tell if the moon is happy?

See if it's beaming!

48.

What happened to the silly alien that wondered where our sun had gone?

By the next morning it had dawned on him!

49.
How do comets greet each other?

Pleased to meteor!

50.
What did the mother star say to the child star?

You shouldn't be out at night!

51.
What did the boy say when the teacher asked which was nearer - India or the Moon?

The moon, because you never see India - but you can see the moon at night!

52.
Why should you never go to a theater on the moon?

It lacks atmosphere!

53.
What's the daftest thing you can see at night?

A fool moon!

54.
What did the boy say when the teacher asked - what do you see at planetariums?

Starfish!

55.

What kind of star always ends up in jail?

A shooting star!

56.

Which of the Star Wars characters gradually disappeared?

Darth Fader!

57.

Which of the Star Wars characters liked to wander up to his thighs in rivers?

Darth Wader!

58.

What did the Emperor say when asked to pay the waitress for lunch?

Darth Paid-her!

59.

When is it difficult to get on the moon?

When it is full!

60.

How do aliens like their cups of tea?

On flying saucers!

61.
What drink don't spacemen have in outer space?

Gravi-tea!

62.
Why do scientists believe there is life on Mars?

Someone stole the wheels off the Mars Rover!

63.
Where do aliens go for their holidays?

Earth – for their annual trip around the Sun!

64.

Why did the sun go to school and then college?

It wanted to be brighter!

65.

What kind of mad insect lives on the moon?

A luna-tic!

66.

What is the cow's favorite object in space?

The Mooooon!

67.
What do astronauts read to enjoy themselves?

Comet books!

68.
What do you press on a keyboard to launch a rocket?

The spacebar!

69.
What was Mickey Mouse doing on Neptune?

Looking for Pluto!

70.

What do you do if you find a space man?

Park in it... man!

71.

Why are astronauts careful when cooking meals?

In case they see an unidentified frying object!

72.

Why is it difficult to keep your job if you're an astronaut?

They are always getting fired!

73.

How do we know astronauts are angry all the time?

They are always blasting off!

74.

What do you get if you cross a student and an alien?

Something from another universe -ity!

75.

Why are spacemen so successful?

They are always going up in the world!

76.

How do galaxies hold up their trousers?

With asteroid belts!

77.

What do cartoon characters living on the moon enjoy watching?

Luna Tunes!

78.

What lights spin around the Earth?

Satel-lites!

79.

What meteorites get their sums wrong at school?

Meteo-wrongs!

80.

How does the moon get his hair cut?

Eclipse it!

81.

Why don't aliens eat in restaurants?

Once they've eaten the waiter there is no-one left to bring their main meal!

82.

What game should you never play with 10 feet tall aliens?

Squash!

83.

How do aliens like to cook humans?

Terror-fried!

84.

What did the alien wear in summer?

Three pairs of sunglasses - one for each head!

85.

What happens if a two ton alien sits on your piano?

You get flat notes!

86.

What happens if you train a two ton alien to walk on a lead?

You'll need to scoop some big poops!

87.

What is an alien's favorite cheese?

Scream cheese!

88.

What's huge with ten arms, twelve legs and goes... Beep! Beep!?

An alien in a traffic jam!

89.

Why did the crazy space alien eat a couch and three chairs?

It had a suite tooth!

90.

How did a hideous alien persuade a pretty girl to kiss it?

With a stun gun!

91.

What's green with five legs and goes up and down, up and down?

An alien stuck in a tractor beam!

92.

Why do aliens wear helmets?

So they don't scare themselves when they look in the mirror!

93.

What do lady aliens with huge teeth do at human parties?

They look for edible bachelors!

94.

What did the man say to the huge alien that wanted to be a train driver?

I won't stand in your way!

95.

How can you tell if you've met a good alien?

You can talk about it later!

96.

What kind of alien spaceship gets upset easily?

A crying saucer!

97.

How do you help a baby astronaut to sleep?

You rock-et!

98.

What did the alien do with the arms that fell off when he grew new ones?

He kept them – he said they might come in handy!

99.

When does the moon stop eating?

When it's full!

100.

What should you do if a huge three headed alien rolls its eyes at you?

Roll them back – quick!

101.

Why was the five-legged alien happy when it came back from the tailors?

Its trousers fitted him like a glove!

101 Monster Jokes for Kids

IP Factly Presents...

1.

What monster is always playing tricks?

Prank-enstein!

2.

What do you call zombies that use phones?

Dead ringers!

3.

What do you call a green monster that you can flick across a room?

The bogey-man!

4.
What did the monster make of her new friends at school?

A pie!

5.
How do you write a report on monsters?

Shave their hair off and tell them to sit very still!

6.
What kind of flour do zombies use to make bread?

Self-raising!

7.

Why didn't the young monster play with the children in the neighborhood?

He wasn't allowed to play with his food!

8.

What happened to the man who crossed a pig with Dracula?

He got a ham-pire!

9.

Why was the monsters' basketball court soaking wet?

They kept dribbling all over it!

10.
How do vampires like their coffee?

De-coffiin-ated!

11.
Why didn't the mummy have friends?

He was too wrapped up in himself!

12.
How do lady vampires attract male vampires?

They bat their eyelashes!

13.

What do vampires enjoy at baseball parks?

Fang-furters!

14.

Why do vampires love baseball?

They enjoy anything with bats in it!

15.

What is a vampire's favorite sport?

Bat-minton!

16.
What other sports do vampires enjoy?

Casketball!

17.
Why was the Cyclops a poor teacher?

He only ever had one pupil!

18.
What happened when the cannibal was an hour late for lunch?

She was given the cold shoulder!

19.

Who did the ghost take to the movies?

His ghoul-friend!

20.

What happened to the man who crossed a vampire with Sir Galahad?

He got a bite in shining armor!

21.

Why did dragons sleep through the day?

So they could fight knights!

22.

How do you stay in touch with famous vampires?

Join their Fang Club!

23.

Where do most American werewolves live?

Hairizona.

24

What sort of band do vampires play in?

A blood group!

25.

Why did the skeleton keep his head in the freezer?

Because he was a numb-skull!

26.

Why are vampires polite when taking blood?

They always *fang* you for it!

27.

How did the young yeti go to school?

On an icicle!

28.

How do lady vampires attract male vampires?

They bat their eyelashes!

29.

Why do vampire films have such large a cast?

For all the bit parts!

30.

How do tired zombies look?

Dead on their feet!

31.

Who is usually the first love for vampires?

The girl necks-door!

32.

Who was the cleverest monster maker ever?

Frank Einstein!

33.

What would you get if you crossed a vampire with a skunk?

I don't know but it would probably get the cinema to itself!

34.

What happened to the man who crossed King Kong and a toad?

He got a giant ape that caught planes with its tongue!

35.

What is fruity and kept in jars to stop them biting?

Jampires!

36.

What did the former werewolf say to the doctor?

I used to be a werewolf but I'm all right nooooooow!

37.

What fruit do vampires love to bite into?

Nectarines!

38.

What monster is 100 meters long, lives in Scotland, and never tidies its room?

The Loch Mess Monster!

39.

Where do vampires eat their school lunches?

At the casket-eria!

40.

What is purple with red spots, 20 legs, huge fangs, and has green goo oozing from its mouth?

I don't know but it's in your hair!

41.

Why are vampires so annoying?

I don't know but they are a pain in the neck!

42.

What's huge with red spots and eats cars?

The greater red-spotted car-eater!

43.

Why do vampires chew gum?

They have bat breath!

44.

What did the little monster say when told to hurry up and tidy its room?

I only have six pairs of hands!

45.

How do vampires keep clean?

They use a bat tub!

46.

Where do monsters keep their hands?

In a box with the rest of the collection!

47.

Why did the vampire go to the doctor?

Because of the coffing!

48.

What is a monster's favorite form of transport?

A chew chew train!

49.
What breed of dog do vampires own?

Blood hounds!

50.
Why were the purple cross-eyed monsters always fighting?

They couldn't see eye to eye over anything!

51.
How did the baker know the vampire had broken in?

All the jelly doughnuts were empty!

52.

Who won the world's first monster beauty contest?

Nobody!

53.

Where do vampires keep their savings?

In a blood bank!

54.

What kind of monsters are the quickest at eating humans?

Goblins!

55.

What sign did the little creature have on his front door?

Gnome Sweet Gnome!

56.

What do vampires take when they catch a cold?

Coffin medicine!

57.

On what day should you expect banshees to start screeching?

Moanday!

58.
What happens to vampires when they get tired?

They end up in a bat temper!

59.
What happened to the man who crossed a hideous three-headed monster with an alarm clock?

He got a very ugly awakening!

60.
What are single male vampires called?

Bat-chelors!

61.

How do we know the monster found Baron Frankenstein funny?

He had him in stitches!

62.

How do vampires say goodbye?

So long sucker!

63.

How do male monsters know they've met their future wife?

It's always love at first fright!

64.

Do monsters think they should eat chicken with their fingers?

No, they have fingers before the chicken!

65.

What did the vampire say after having work done on his teeth?

Fang-tastic!

66.

What happened to the monster that had burglars one night?

He had beans on toast the next night!

67.

What do vampires sometimes do for special occasions?

Club together and get a giraffe!

68.

What happened when the monster brought his friend home for dinner?

He went well with fries!

69.

What do vampire teachers do at recess?

Take a coffin break!

70.

How did the monster mother stop her son smelling?

She pulled off his nose!

71.

What do you call a mad vampire?

Batty!

72.

What is a monster's favorite game at school?

Swallow the leader!

73.

Where do you find the most vampires in New York?

The Vampire State Building!

74.

What happened when the police said they were looking for a monster with one eye called Cyclops!

Everyone wanted to know what the other eye was called!

75.

How do vampires cross the ocean?

On blood vessels!

76.

What is hairy with five legs and can disappear into a cloud?

A monster jumping out of a plane!

77.

What do vampires do at blood banks?

Ask to make a withdrawal!

78.

What did the headstone for Frankenstein's monster say?

Rest in Pieces!

79.

What are dumb vampires that can't suck blood properly called?

Blood clots!

80.

What happened to the old monster with the face of an eighteen-year old?

He had to give it back!

81.

What superhero do vampires like the best?

Bat-man!

82.

Why was Baron Frankenstein good around strangers?

He could make friends easily!

83.

How do baby vampires like their food?

In bite-sized pieces!

84.

What happened to the man who crossed huge monsters with pigeons?

He got a lot of very messy statues!

85.

Why do baby vampires not drink milk?

They like something they can sink their teeth into!

86.

What's the best way to help starving monsters?

Give them a hand!

87.

Why are vampires sometimes taken advantage of?

Because they are suckers!

88.

What kind of monsters only eats your mother's sister?

Aunt-eaters!

89.

What kind of dance do vampires enjoy?

The fang-dango!

90.

How did Frankenstein's monster wake up?

Bolt upright!

91.
What do monsters call skateboarders?

Meals on wheels!

92.
When is a vampire most likely to bite you?

On Chewsdays!

93.
Why haven't monster eaten Usain Bolt yet?

He'd give them the runs!

94.
When do monsters only eat children?

When they are on a diet!

95.
What do you call ghost mistakes?

Boo-Boos!

96.
Why do vampires never win 100m sprints?

They always finish neck and neck!

97.

What happened when Baron Frankenstein saw a bare-necked corpse walking around?

He made a bolt for it!

98.

What do vampires sing at New Year?

Auld Fang Syne!

99.

Why do ghouls and demons spend all their time together?

Because demons are a ghouls best friend!

100.

What moves oxygen around zombie blood?

Dead blood cells!

101.

What do you call vampires in the mafia?

Fangsters!

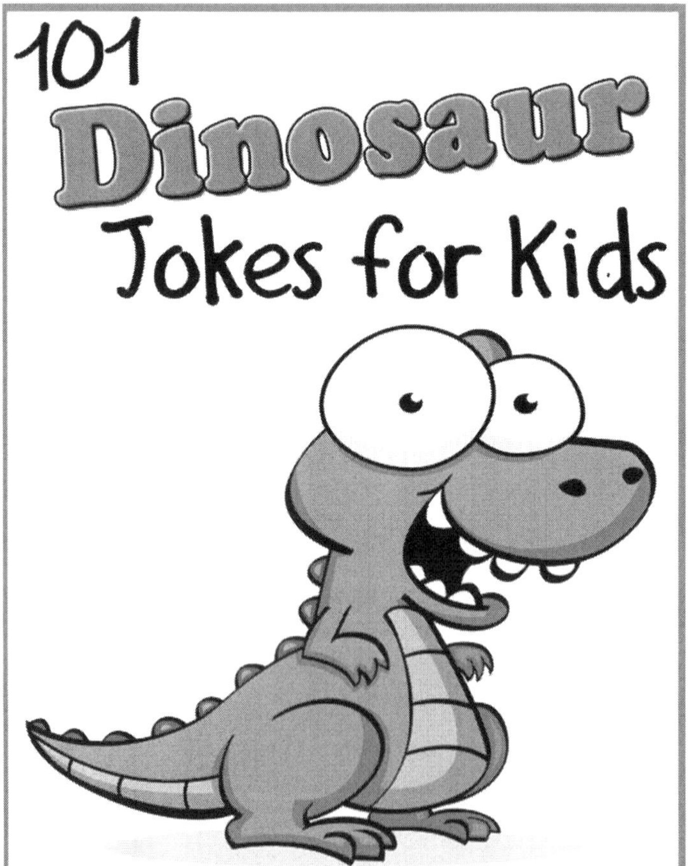
101
Dinosaur
Jokes for Kids
IP Factly Presents...

1.

What kind of dinosaurs used to suddenly burst?

Tricera-pops!

2.

What kind of dinosaurs made the best police?

Tricera-cops!

3.

What did dinosaurs use to cut down trees?

Dino-saws!

4.

What happened to the man who crossed a T-Rex with a chicken?

He got tyrannosaurus pecks!

5.

What kind of dinosaur was always crashing trucks?

Tyrannosaurus wrecks!

6.

Why did the dinosaur cross the road?

The chicken hadn't evolved yet!

7.

Why did the dinosaur stop before crossing the road?

It was waiting for someone to invent asphalt!

8.

What dinosaur had the worst vision?

Tyrannosaurus specs!

9.

What dinosaurs were good at soccer?

Dino-scores!

10.
What kind of dinosaur never gives in?

Try-try-try-again-ceratops!

11.
Why did the Archaeopteryx catch the worm?

It was an early bird!

12.
Which dinosaur ate the best food in the Southern USA?

Tyrannosaurus Tex-Mex!

13.

What kind of dinosaurs slept all the time?

Dino-snores!

14.

What kind of dinosaurs were the best triple jumpers?

Tricera-hops!

15.

What kind of dinosaurs lived high up in mountains?

Tricera-tops!

16.

What dinosaur has a very firm handshake?

Grip-lodocus!

17.

What was the best of the kissing dinosaurs?

Lip-lodocus!

18.

What do you call fossils that stay in river beds all day?

Lazy bones!

19.
What kind of dinosaur was always hurting itself?

Really-saurus!

20.
What kind of dinosaurs never shut up?

Dino-bores!

21.
What happened to the man who crossed a rope with a dinosaur?

He got a skip-lodocus!

22.

What dinosaur only drinks small amounts of water at a time?

Sip-lodocus!

23.

What kind of dinosaurs appeared in cowboy films?

Tyrannosaurus tex!

24.

What dinosaur often appeared at rodeos?

Bucking bronco-saurus!

25.

What kind of dinosaur had no eyes?

It-never-saurus!

26.

What kind of dinosaur had no eyes but did have a pet dog?

It-never-saurus rex!

27.

What was the most explosive of all the dinosaurs?

Dino-mites!

28.

What happened to the man who crossed a T-Rex with the floor of a ship?

He got tyrannosaurus decks!

29.

What happened to the man who crossed a T-Rex with a diplodocus?

He got tyrannosaurus necks!

30.

What did the giganotosaurus eat?

Anything it wanted!

31.

What happened to the man who crossed an acrobat with a dinosaur?

He got a flip-lodocus!

32.

What happened to the man who crossed a crab with a dinosaur?

He got a nip-lodocus!

33.

Why did the tyrannosaur walk on two legs?

So it didn't squash the strawberries!

34.

What happened when the tyrannosaur walked through the strawberries?

It got strawberry jam!

35.

What should you do if you find a tyrannosaurus in your kitchen making lunch?

Book a restaurant!

36.

Did dinosaurs take showers?

No, they were always attached to the wall!

37.

What happened to the man who crossed a dinosaur with a snack?

He got a chip-lodocus!

38.

What happened to the man who crossed a leaky faucet with a dinosaur?

He got a drip-lodocus!

39.

What do you find in the middle of dinosaurs?

S!

40.

What happened when dinosaurs took buses?

They had to bring them back!

41.

Why did dinosaurs avoid the sea?

They thought there was something fishy about it!

42.

What happened to the man who crossed a dinosaur with an omelet?

He got an egg-osaurus!

43.

What happened when the iron dinosaur got rained on?

It became a stegosau-rust!

44.

What dinosaur used to put its washing out on the line to dry?

Peg-osaurus!

45.

What dinosaur was tasty and could feed a village?

Chicken-leg-osaurus!

46.

What happened to the man who crossed a tyrannosaurus with the beach?

He got a dino-shore!

47.

Where did the stegosaurus get its groceries?

At the dino-store!

48.

Why did the dinosaur never forget to lock its front door?

Because tyrannosaurus checks!

49.

What happened to the man who crossed a dinosaur with a coach?

Tyrannosaur-bus?

50.

What dinosaur is the best at math?

Tyrannosaur-plus?

51.

What did baby tyrannosaurus like to play on at the park?

A dino-see-saur!

52.

Who kind of dinosaur mends clothing?

A dino-sewer!

53.

Why didn't dinosaurs have police?

They couldn't fit in the uniforms!

54.

Why didn't dinosaurs have long hair?

They had good barbers!

55.
What dinosaur never told the truth?

Lie-ceratops!

56.
What dinosaur was always asking questions?

Why-ceratops!

57.
Why did dinosaurs have wrinkled skin?

They spent too long in the bath!

58.

Why did dinosaurs paint themselves black and white and jump in rivers?

To confuse the crocodiles!

59.

Why did the brontosaurus wear dark glasses?

To avoid being recognized!

60.

What was the saddest dinosaur?

Cry-ceratops!

61.

Which was the first of the dinosaurs to go extinct?

Die-ceratops!

62.

Why do museums have old dinosaur bones?

They can't afford new ones!

63.

What do you say to a thirsty tyrannosaur?

Tea, Rex?

64.

How can you tell how old a dinosaur is?

By the candles on its cake!

65.

What happened to the man who cooked a dinosaur in pastry?

He got a pie-ceratops!

66.

What was the best dressed dinosaur?

Suit and tie-ceratops!

67.

Why did tyrannosaurs never cook their meat on a fire?

They could never reach the matches in their pocket!

68.

Where do you find dinosaur words?

In a thesaurus!

69.

How do we know dinosaurs lack of showers led to their demise?

They ended up ex-stinked!

70.
What was the dinosaur's favorite meal?

Jurassic pork!

71.
Why kind of tyrannosaur always got rained on?

A dino-pour!

72.
What kind of dinosaurs were used to clean up?

Tricera-mops!

73.
What was the tidiest dinosaur?

A cleaner-saurus!

74.
What kind of dinosaurs used to like buying clothes?

Tricera-shops!

75.
What kind of dinosaur did secret work for the army?

Tricera-special-ops!

76.

What kind of dinosaur was the most accident prone?

A break-iosaurus!

77.

What happened to the man who crossed a dinosaur with a leg?

He got a thigh-ceratops!

78.

Why didn't the dinosaur like meeting other dinosaurs?

It was a shy-ceratops!

79.

How did the last of the dinosaurs pass their exams?

With extinctions!

80.

What time is it when velociraptors call round for tea?

Time to escape by the backdoor!

81.

What kind of dinosaur kept everyone up all night?

The bronta-snorer!

82.

What happened to the man who crossed a dinosaur with a bluebottle?

He got a fly-ceratops!

83.

What happened to the man who crossed a dinosaur with a mountain?

He got a high-ceratops!

84.

Why did the man keep finding dinosaurs in his garden?

Because they were terrible at hide and seek!

85.

Why are dinosaur bones always found in the ground?

They didn't climb trees!

86.

Why does no-one ever hear pterodactyls using the bathroom?

Because they have a silent P!

87.

What kind of dinosaur loves to read?

A veloci-chapter!

88.

What kind of dinosaur loves to cook burgers?

Fry-ceratops!

89.

What did triceratops sit on?

Tricera-bottoms!

90.

What did the triceratops play in the school band?

The horn!

91.

What do you call an underwater tyrannosaurus?

A diver-saur!

92.

What do you call a NASCAR racing tyrannosaurus?

A driver-saur!

93.

How do you keep a brontosaurus and a diplodocus under an umbrella without getting wet?

Make sure it's not raining!

94.

How can you tell if your mum keeps dinosaurs in the refrigerator?

The door won't shut!

95.

What happened to the man who crossed a T-Rex with a place to eat?

He got a diner-saur!

96.

What happened to the man who crossed a T-Rex with a poet?

He got a rhymer-soar!

97.
What do you call a dinosaur puppy?

Rex!

98.
What's worse than a giraffe with tonsillitis?

A brontosaurus with a sore throat!

99.
Where did the tyrannosaurus' poop go?

The dino-sewer!

100.

What do you call a velociraptor made from building blocks?

A lego-saur!

101.

Why didn't dinosaurs climb trees?

They couldn't build treehouses!

101 Wild Animal Jokes for Kids

IP Factly Presents...

1.

What do you call an exploding ape?

A baboom!

2.

What animal is always coming back to life?

Frogs, they croak all the time!

3.

What do you call an alligator that steals things?

A crook-odile!

4.

What do you call a monkey with a wizard's hat and a broomstick?

Hairy Potter!

5.

How do apes get around the jungle?

In hot air baboons!

6.

What is a polar bear's favorite meal?

Ice berg-ers!

7.

What is big, muddy and sends people into a trance?

A hypno-potamus!

8.

What do you call a tiger that ate your father's sister?

An aunt-eater!

9.

When are you most likely to be eaten by a tiger?

Chewsday!

10.

What is tasty and lives in trees?

A meringue-utan!

11.

What do you call a baby hippo that can't use the bathroom properly?

A hippo-potty-mess!

12.

What did the adult snake say to the baby snake with a runny nose?

Viper your nose!

13.

What fruit do monkeys like to eat?

Ape-les!

14.

What do gorillas wear in the kitchen?

Ape-rons!

15.

Where is a baboon's favorite fruit?

Ape-ricots!

16.

What apes always come back no matter how hard you throw them?

Baboon-erangs!

17.

Why did the viper not viper nose?

Because the adder, adder tissue!

18.

How do rabbits go on vacation?

By hare-plane!

19.

What is an ape's favorite snack?

Chocolate chimp cookies!

20.

What's an old bear with no teeth called?

Gummy bear!

21.

Why do male deer always need braces?

They have buck teeth!

22.

What did the ape say when it missed the phone call?

Who-rang-utang!

23.

How many skunks do you need to stink out a shopping mall?

Quite a phew!

24.

How do bears keep cool in summer?

They have bear conditioning!

25.
How do you catch a squirrel?

Sit on a branch and act like a nut!

26.
How can you catch a monkey?

Sit on a branch and act like a banana!

27.
What do you do to find a lost monkey?

Sit on a branch and make a noise like a banana!

28.

Why should you be careful playing cards in Africa?

There are lots of cheetahs.

29.

Why did the snake cross the road?

To get to the other sssssside!

30.

How do you send messages in the forest?

Moss code.

31.

What is black, white and red all over?

An embarrassed zebra.

32.

What is black, white with a purple face?

A zebra holding his breath!

33.

What happened when the tiger ate the joke book?

He felt funny!

34.

What is small, cuddly and highly dangerous?

A koala with a rocket launcher!

35.

What do you get if you cross a snake and a pie?

A pie-thon!

36.

What game does a crocodile love to play?

Snap!

37.

What do lions say before they go hunting?

Let us prey!

38.

What is a snake's favorite dance?

The mamba!

39.

What kind of bears like light rain showers?

Drizzly bears!

40.

Why did St. Patrick drive all the snakes out of Ireland?

It was too far to walk!

41.

What is a snake's favorite subject at school?

Hiss-tory!

42.

Why do koalas never wear socks?

They prefer bear feet!

43.

What snake might you use when driving?

A windshield viper!

44.

Why was the leopard wearing a striped jumper?

So he wouldn't be spotted!

45.

What steps should you take if you a lion is charging towards you?

Big ones!

46.

What kind of butterfly should you be scared of?

A tiger moth!

47.

Where does a 1,000 pound gorilla sit?

Wherever it wants!

48.

What do you call a 1,000 pound gorilla?

Whatever it wants!

49.

What did the buffalo say to his child on the first day of school?

Bi-son!

50.

How do you stop a skunk smelling?

Give it a nose plug!

51.

What animal is striped and bouncy?

A tiger on a trampoline!

52.

What do you call bears without any ears?

B!

53.

What happened to the man who crossed a pig with a bear?

He got a teddy boar!

54.

How does a lion greet other animals at the watering hole?

Pleased to eat you!

55.

What do porcupines like to eat?

Prickled cucumber!

56.

What happened to the leopard that stayed in the bath for a month?

It came out spotless!

57.

What happened when a man tried to cross a tiger with a sheep?

He had to get a new sheep!

58.

What do chimps say to baby chimps when they fall over?

Apesy-daisy!

59.

How did the mouse save its drowning friend?

It used mouse to mouse resuscitation!

60.

Why do monkeys climb trees?

The elevators are always broken!

61.
How do you make a buffalo stew?

Keep it waiting for an hour!

62.
Why did the boy keep oiling the rat?

Because it wouldn't stop squeaking!

63.
How do you make a purple monkey?

Cross a red monkey with a blue one!

64.

What happened to the man who crossed a Lego set with a snake?

He got a boa constructor!

65.

How do monkeys use stairs?

They slide down the banana-ster!

66.

Which animals shout when trees are chopped down?

Timberrrr wolves!

67.
Why are baby snakes always so happy?

They come with their own rattle!

68.
What did the rats play at recess?

Hide and squeak!

69.
What is black, white, red and spotty?

A skunk with chicken pox!

70.

Why don't snakes use weighing machines?

They have their own scales!

71.

Why are leopards so bad at hide and seek?

They are always spotted!

72.

How do you begin a bear race?

Ready, teddy, go!

73.
What do snakes write in valentine cards?

Love and hisses...!

74.
What happens if you cross a bear with a skunk?

You get Winnie the Pooheeey!

75.
What do you get if you cross a pig, a snake and a builder?

A boar constructor!

76.

If crocodiles are used for shoes what are used for slippers?

Bananas!

77.

Why are wolves like cards?

You'll always find them in packs!

78.

What did the boa constrictor say to the mouse?

I've got a crush on you!

79.

Why was the alligator coughing?

It had a frog in its throat!

80.

Why do bears have fur coats?

Because they tried macs and they looked silly.

81.

What did the snake say when the teacher asked him a question?

Don't asp me!

82.

What's the name for a group of lions taking it in turns to use a copy machine?

Copy cats!

83.

What do you give an ill viper?

Asp-rin!

84.

Why are penguins cheap to keep?

They live on ice!

85.
What happened to the man who crossed a new born snake with a trampoline?

He got a bouncing baby boa!

86.
How do you hire a porcupine?

Put it on a box!

87.
Which snakes are the best at math?

Adders!

88.
What is brown, rattles and says, "hith" "hith"?

A rattlesnake with a lisp!

89.
Why did the igloo not have a couch?

So polar bears couldn't hide behind it!

90.
What did the snail on the turtle's shell say?

Weeeeee!

91.

Why did the ape try to cook on his head?

He thought he was a griller!

92.

How much does a male deer cost?

A buck!

93.

What did a judge say to a skunk in the dock?

Odor in the court!

94.
How do apes open bananas?

They use mon-keys!

95.
What happened when 100 hares escaped from prison?

Police had to comb the area!

96.
Where do monkeys get all their gossip?

On the 'ape-vine!

97.

Why did the otter cross the road?

To get to the otter side!

98.

How do camels hide in the jungle?

They use camel-flage!

99.

Which show always leaves leopards out of breath?

The Pink Panter Show!

100.

Which hand should you always use to stroke a lion?

Someone else's!

101.

What should you do if you find a tiger in your bathroom?

Wait till he's finished!

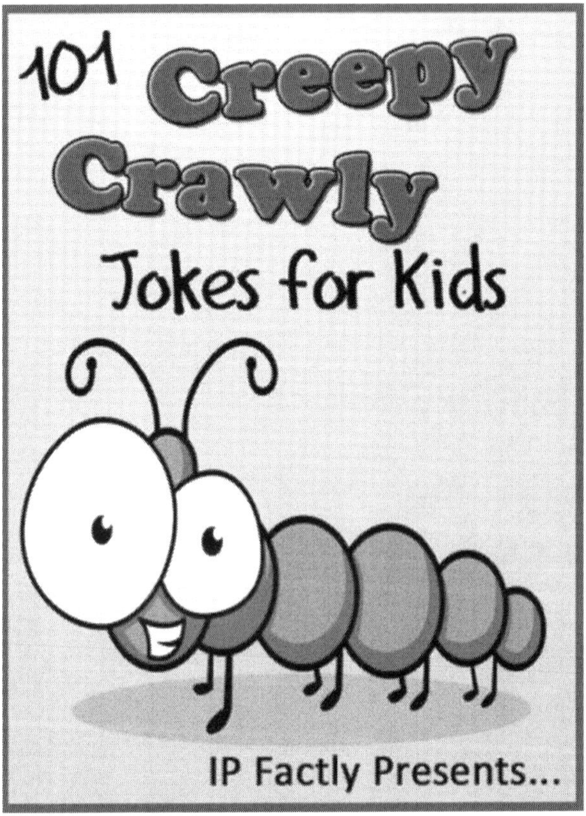
101 Creepy Crawly
Jokes for Kids
IP Factly Presents...

1.

How can you tell which end of a worm is the head?

Tickle it in the middle and see which end laughs!

2.

What goes zzub, zzub?

A bee flying backwards!

3.

How do the police scare bugs away?

They call for the S.W.A.T. team!

4.

How do you catch a bee bus?

Wait at a buzz stop!

5.

How can you recognize police glow worms?

They have blue lights!

6.

What do bees love to chew?

Bumble gum!

7.

What has antlers and sucks blood?

A moose-quito!

8.

What does a queen bee do when she burps?

Issues a royal pardon!

9.

Why was the centipede dropped from the insect football team?

He took too long putting his boots on!

10.

What kind of bee is difficult to understand?

A mumble bee!

11.

What do you call a mosquito in a metal suit?

A bite in shining armor!

12.

What is worse than finding a worm in your apple?

Finding half a worm!

13.

What do you get if you cross lots of ants and tics?

All sorts of antics!

14.

What did an early worm say to the late worm?

Where in earth have you been!

15.

What is the definition of a slug?

A homeless snail!

16.

What do you call an ant that dodges school?

A tru-ant!

17.

Where do you find giant snails?

At the end of giant's fingers!

18.

What do you call a well-dressed ant?

Eleg-ant!

19.

Why did the queen bee kick out all of the other bees ?

Because they kept droning on and on!

20.

Where do ants go for dinner?

A restaur-ant!

21.

Why wouldn't they let the butterfly into the dance?

It was a moth ball!

22.
Where do bees go on holiday?

Stingapore!

23.
What's smaller than an ant's mouth?

An ant's lunch!

24.
Why did the wood worm spend most of his time alone?

Because he was always boring!

25.
Why are mosquitos religious?

They prey on you!

26.
What size meals do glow worms prefer?

Light meals

27.
How do bees get to school?

School buzz!

28.

How do you make a glow worm laugh?

Cut off his tail, he'll be de-lighted!

29.

What was the snail doing on the highway?

About one mile a week!

30.

What's the difference between spiders now and twenty years ago?

Spiders used to have webs now they have websites!

31.

Why should you always keep glow worms in your bag?

They lighten your load!

32.

What lives in gum trees?

Mint flavored stick insects!

33.

What did the cop slug say to the escaping robber slug?

I'll get you next slime!

34.
Why do bees have sticky hair?

Because they use honeycombs!

35.
How do stones stop moths eating your clothes?

Because rolling stones gather no moths!

36.
What do caterpillars do on New Year's Day?

Turn over a new leaf!

37.

What is the difference between a mosquito and a fly?

Try unzipping a mosquito!

38.

Which insect directs films?

Steven Speilbug!

39.

What do you do when two snails fight?

Leave them to slug it out!

40.

Why did the firefly keep stealing things?

He was light fingered!

41.

What did one firefly say to the other?

Got to glow now!

42.

What did the squeaky-clean dog say to the bug?

Long time no flea!

43.
How do you know your kitchen floor is dirty?

The slugs leave a trail saying "clean me!"

44.
What do frogs order when they go out for lunch?

French Flies!

45.
What do you call a snail on a ship?

A snailor!

46.

What do you call a rabbit with fleas?

Bugs Bunny!

47.

What do you get if you cross a centipede and a parrot?

A walkie-talkie!

48.

Who make dogs itch and humans laugh?

The Flea Stooges!

49.

How do snails get their shells so shiny?

They use snail varnish!

50.

Why did the fly never land on the computer?

It was afraid of websites!

51.

Why was the glow-worm confused?

It didn't know if it was coming or glowing!

52.
How does a flea travel?

They 'itch-hike!

53.
What is the difference between school dinners and a load of slugs?

School dinners come on a plate!

54.
What do you call a clever glow-worm?

A bright spark!

55.

What do you call a fly with no wings?

A walk!

56.

What do you get when you cross a walrus with a bee?

A wallaby!

57.

Why didn't the two worms go on Noah's Ark in an apple?

Because they all had to go on in pairs!

58.
Why was the baby ant confused?

Because all his uncles were ants!

59.
Why did the kid throw the butter up in the air?

To see the butter fly!

60.
What did the bees from Canada say to their cousins in Florida?

Swarm here isn't it!

61.

What has 50 legs but can't walk?

Half a centipede!

62.

What is a baby bee?

A little humbug!

63.

What is the difference between a flea and a wolf?

One prowls on the hairy and the other howls on the prairie!

64.
Why was the millipede late?

Because he was playing "This little Piggy" with his baby sister!

65.
What do you call an ant with frog's legs?

An ant-phibian!

66.
Where do bees save their money?

In a honey box!

67.
What is even bigger than an elephant?

A gi-ant!

68.
What kind of fast food do bees like?

Humburgers!

69.
What do you get if you cross a centipede and a chicken?

Enough drumsticks to feed a whole town!

70.

What do you call an ant that likes to be alone?

Independ-ant!

71.

What do you call a bee born in May?

A maybe!

72.

What kind of wig can hear?

An earwig!

73.

How do you start an insect race?

One, two, flea - go!

74.

How do you start a firefly race?

Ready steady glow!

75.

How do you find where a flea bit your dog?

Start from scratch!

76.

How do you keep flies out of the kitchen?

Let your dog poop in the living room!

77.

What goes "snap, crackle and pop"?

A firefly with a short circuit!

78.

What insect is good for your health?

Vitamin bee!

79.

What has 6 legs, sucks blood, and talks in code?

A morse-quito!

80.

What do butterflies learn at school?

Moth-matics!

81.

What goes buzz... choo! Buzz... choo!?

A bee with hay fever!

82.

What's the biggest moth in the world?

A mam-moth!

83.

What do you call a guard with 100 legs?

A sentrypede!

84.

What has four wheels and flies?

A trash can!

85.

How do you save an injured insect?

Call an ant-bulance!

86.

What did the spider say to the fly?

I'm getting married do you want to come to the webbing?

87.

What kind of bees are always dropping things?

Fumble bees!

88.
Why are spiders like tops?

They are always spinning!

89.
What do you call a bee that's had a spell put on it?

Bee-witched!

90.
What do you call an ant with five pairs of eyes?

Antteneye!

91.

What did the bee say to a naughty bee?

Bee-hive yourself!

92.

What kind of ant is good at maths?

An account-ant!

93.

How does a queen bee move around?

She's throne!

94.

What's even more dangerous than being with a fool?

Fooling with a bee!

95.

What do you call a 100 year old ant?

An ant-ique!

96.

Why was the sparrow in the library?

It was looking for bookworms!

97.

What do you call an ant that lives with your great uncle?

Your great-ant!

98.

What did the woodworm say to the table?

It's been nice gnawing you!

99.

What is the biggest ant in the world?

An eleph-ant!

100.

Why was the glow worm unhappy?

She realized she wasn't that bright!

101.

Who was the most famous ant scientist?

Albert Ant-stein!

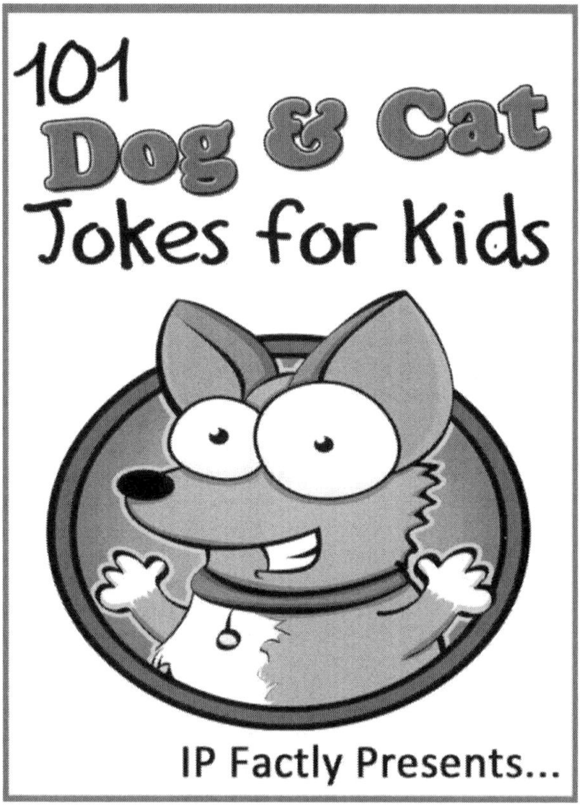
101
Dog & Cat
Jokes for Kids
IP Factly Presents...

1.
How do cats freshen their breath?

Mouse-wash!

2.
What dogs make the best hairdressers?

Shampoodles!

3.
What kind of dog goes tick, tick, woof, woof, tick, tick, woof, woof?

A watch dog!

4.

What kind of cat loves duck burgers?

A duck-filled patty puss!

5.

What animal has even more lives than a cat?

A toad - it is always croaking!

6.

What do nursing cats always carry?

First aid kit-tens!

7.

Why do you have to be careful when it starts raining cats and dogs?

You might step in a poodle!

8.

What do cats enjoy at breakfast?

Mice Krispies!

9.

Why don't cats and dogs dance together?

They both have two left feet!

10.

What warning sound do Australian dogs on bicycles make?

Dingo-ling!

11.

What happened to the man who crossed his dog with a tiger?

He had fewer friends visiting!

12.

What do you get if you cross a black dog and a white dog?

A greyhound!

13.
What is black and white and purple?

A Dalmatian holding its breath!

14.
What animal do cats like to sleep on?

A caterpillows!

15.
What happened to the little dog that met a lion?

He was terrier-fied!

16.
What did the dog say when it sat on some bark?

Ruff!

17.
Why do cats always have high scores on video games?

They have nine lives!

18.
Why are postal workers afraid of dogs called Frost?

Because Frost-bites!

19.

What dogs rip the mail every morning?

Tear-riers!

20.

What happened to the man who crossed his dog with an elephant?

I can't recall - but ask the elephant it'll remember!

21.

Why do dogs scratch themselves?

No-one else knows where the itch is!

22.

What kind of dog wears dark glasses and likes riding motorcycles?

A police dog!

23.

When would it be unlucky to see a black cat?

If you were a mouse!

24.

Boy: I lost my dog!

Father: Maybe you could put an ad in the paper?

Boy: That would be no good – he can't read!

25.

Girl: My cat swallowed a ball of wool!

Teacher: Oh no! What happened?

Girl: She had mittens!

26.

What are caterpillars' worst enemies?

Dog-erpillars!

27.

Why can't you train cats?

Because they think they are already purr-fect!

28.

Why don't you need a license for a cat?

You can't teach cats to lie down – you could never teach them to drive!

29.

What happened to the man who crossed a dog and a sheep?

He got a sheep that could herd itself!

30.

Why did the chihuahua bite the policeman's foot?

That was as far as it could reach!

31.

When should you take a pit bull terrier for a walk?

Whenever it wants!

32.

What was the greatest dog detective called?

Sherlock Bones!

33.

Why do dogs bury bones in the back yard?

Because they are not allowed to bury them in the kitchen!

34.

Why are big trees and little dogs similar?

They both have lots of bark!

35.

What kind of cat can perform somersaults and handstands?

An acro-cat!

36.

Where did the pit bull terrier sit at the movies?

Anywhere it wanted!

37.

What happened to the man that crossed a plane with a dog?

He found himself a jet setter!

38.

How do you know a dog eating fireflies is happy?

It barks with de-light!

39.

What do young dogs buy at a drive-in?

Pup-corn!

40.

What item from the bakery do young dogs love?

Pup-cakes!

41.

How do dogs stop the music?

They press the paws button!

42.

What did the dog say when it sat on a fallen tree?

Bark!

43.

How do you stop a dog digging?

Take away its shovel!

44.

Which dogs live in volcanoes?

Hot dogs!

45.

What is a young dog's favorite snack?

Pup-tarts!

46.
What is a young dog's favorite pizza topping?

Pup-peroni!

47.
What is a cat's favorite car?

Cat-illac!

48.
What cat purrs the most?

Purr-sian!

49.

What happened to the man who crossed a cat and a gorilla?

He got an animal that put him out at night!

50.
What kind of cats are disasters waiting to happen?

Cat-astrophes!

51.
What kind of cat loves mail order magazines?

A cat-alog!

52.

What happened to the man who crossed a dog with a lion?

He got an animal that barks at zebras!

53.

What kind of cat has eight legs and squirts ink?

An octo-puss!

54.

What happened to the man who crossed a cat with a lemon?

He ended up with a sourpuss!

55.

What kind of dancing do young dogs like best?

Body-pupping

56.

How do young dogs keep cool in the summer?

They lick ice pups!

57.

What happened to the man who crossed a cat with the New York Times?

He got a mews-paper!

58.

How can you spell mousetrap with only three letters?

C-A-T!

59.

What happened to the man who crossed a cat with knee-length shoes?

He got puss in boots!

60.

When does a cat go "woof"?

When learning a new language!

61.

How do you know your dog's been chasing ducks?

He's down in the mouth!

62.

How do you catch stray dogs?

Lie down and pretend you are a bone!

63.

What was the cat doing with cheese on its tongue and its mouth wide open?

Waiting with baited breath!

64.

What did the man say about the dog fed on rotten meat, garlic and old cheese?

Its bark is a lot worse than its bite!

65.

What do you call young dogs playing in melting snow?

Slush puppies!

66.

How did the dog untidy the house?

With a litter of puppies!

67.

What happened to the man who crossed a pit bull terrier and a seeing-eye dog?

It bit him then helped him across the road to the hospital!

68.

What do dogs do as a hobby?

Flea collecting!

69.

What do cats always watch at night?

The ten o'clock mews!

70.

What happened to the man who crossed his dog with a frog?

He got licked from across the room!

71.

What do dumb dogs do?

Chase parked cars!

72.

What happened to the man who crossed his dog with a cheetah?

It chased cars and caught them!

73.

At what kind of market might a dog pick up something new?

A flea market!

74.

What happened when the man crossed his dog with a forest?

There was a lot of bark-ing!

75.

What did the dog get at dog school when it had to take six from nine?

Flea!

76.

What did the dog say at dog school when asked to take six from six?

Nothing!

77.

What do alley cats like to do on a Friday night?

Go bowling!

78.

What do dogs become after they are 12 years old?

13 years old!

79.

What kind of dog always knows the time?

A watch dog!

80.

What did the dog say to the cat prancing across its yard?

Nothing, dogs can't talk!

81.

Why does a dog get so hot at the beach?

It wears a coat and pants!

82.

How can you tell the difference between a suit and a dog?

A suit is jacket and pants but a dog just pants!

83.

What's even worse than raining cats and dogs?

Hailing taxis!

84.

How do dogs like their eggs?

Pooched!

85.

What did the cat get after visiting the doctor?

A purr-scription!

86.

What is the favorite color of a cat?

Purr-ple!

87.

Where do you take a legless dog?

For a drag!

88.

What should you do when your dog chews a dictionary?

Take the words out of its mouth!

89.

What happened to the man who crossed roses and dogs?

He got a bumper crop of collie-flowers!

90.

What happened to the man who crossed a dog with a killer whale?

He got an animal that barks at sharks!

91.

What happened to the man who crossed his dog with a car?

He kept it in a barking lot!

92.

What is noisier than your neighbor's dog barking?

Four of your neighbor's dogs barking!

93.

What happened to the man who crossed a cat and a canary?

He got shredded tweet!

94.

What is the first thing a dog does when it jumps in a lake?

Gets wet!

95.

Which US state has the most cats and dogs?

Pet-sylvania!

96.

Why do dogs always run in circles?

Because they don't know how many sides a rectangle has!

97.

What kind of dog should you use to find flowers in spring?

A bud-hound!

98.

What is a vampire's favorite dog?

A bloodhound!

99.

What goes Miaooooooooow?

A cat on a motorcycle!

100.
How much is cat food?

$2 purr can!

101.
Why do dogs wag their tail?

No-one else will do it!

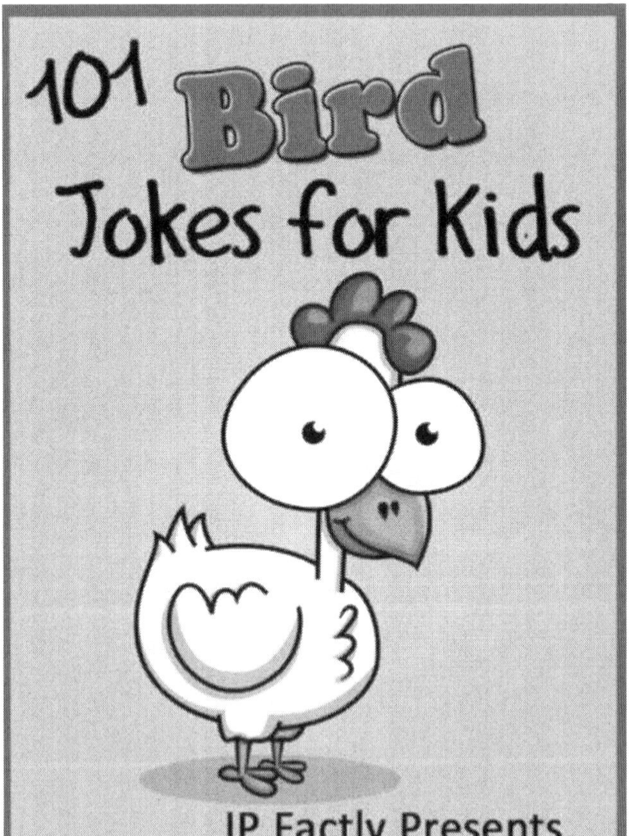
101 Bird
Jokes for Kids
IP Factly Presents...

1.

How did the bird with a broken wing manage to land safely?

It used its sparrow-chute!

2.

Why did the bird go to the gift shop?

Because he wanted a tweet!

3.

What birds spend Sunday on their knees?

Birds of prey!

4.

How do chickens get strong?

Egg-cersize!

5.

What do you call an ostrich at the South Pole?

Lost!

6.

What did one duck egg say to the other duck egg?

Let's get quacking!

7.

What book tells you all about chickens?

A hen-cyclopedia!

8.

When does a duck wake up?

At the quack of dawn!

9.

How does a penguin make pancakes?

With its flippers!

10.

What bird will steal soap from the bath?

A robber duck!

11.

What do you call a crazy chicken?

A cuckoo cluck!

12.

How do you know a duck enjoys flying upside down?

It quacks up!

13.

What does a confused hen lay?

Scrambled eggs!

14.

What do you call a crate full of ducks?

A box of quackers!

15.

What's a haunted chicken?

A poultry-geist!

16.

If apples and pears come from fruit trees, where do ducks and chickens come from?

Poul-trees!

17.

What do you get if you cross a shark with a parrot?

An animal that can talk your head off!

18.

What do you get if you cross a canary and a 20-foot snake?

A sing-a-long!

19.
What said "quick, quick"?

A duck with hiccups!

20.
How do you catch a unique bird?

Unique up on it!

21.
How do you catch a tame bird?

The tame way, unique up on it!

22.
What do you call a bird in winter?

Brrr-d!

23.
Why are pelican doctors so expensive?

Because of the big bills!

24.
What kind of bird works at a construction site?

A crane!

25.

Why do hummingbirds hum?

They can't remember the words!

26.

Why do flamingos lift up one leg?

Because if they lifted both legs they would fall over!

27.

What is even smarter than a talking bird?

A spelling bee!

28.

What do you get when you cross a parrot with a centipede?

A walkie-talkie!

29.

Why do seagulls fly over the sea?

Because if they flew over the bay they would be called bagels!

30.

What would you see at a chicken show?

Hen-tertainment!

31.

What did the duck say when it finished shopping?

Put it on my bill!

32.

What did one chicken say to the other after they ate some poison ivy?

You scratch my beak and I'll scratch yours!

33.

Which birds are from Portugal?

Portu-geese!

34.

Which day of the week do chickens hate the most?

Fry-day!

35.

What bird is always with you when you eat?

A swallow!

36.

What do you get if you cross a parrot with a pig?

A bird that hogs the conversation!

37.

Why was the chick disappointed with its life?

It wasn't all it was cracked up to be!

38.

What is the saddest bird in the world?

A bluebird!

39.

Why do poor canaries learn to talk as quick as rich ones?

Because talk is cheep!

40.

Where do birds invest their money?

In the stork market!

41.

What does a cat call a peregrine falcon?

Fast food!

42.

What do you get if you cross a canary and a 50-foot long snake?

A sing-a-long!

43.

Where did the boy think chickens came from?

Eggplants!

44.

What do you call it when it rains chickens and ducks?

Foul weather!

45.

Why don't chickens like humans?

We beat eggs!

46.

What kind of birds do you have to keep locked up?

Jailbirds!

47.

Which side of a chicken has the most feathers?

The outside!

48.

How do you know that owls are cleverer than chickens?

Have you ever heard of Kentucky-fried owl!

49.

What do you call a bird that digs underground?

A mynah bird!

50.

What do you get if you cross a chicken with a cow?

Roost beef!

51.

What is a pigeon's favorite TV show?

The feather forecast!

52.

What was the name of the canary that flew into the pastry dish?

Tweetie Pie!

53.

What's the most musical part of a chicken?

The drumstick!

54.

What do you get if your canary flies into the blender?

Shredded tweet!

55.
What do ducks watch on TV?

Duckumentaries!

56.
When's the best time to buy a bird?

When it's going cheep!

57.
What happened to the chicken whose feathers were all pointing the wrong way?

She was tickled to death!

58.

Where do tough chickens come from?

Hard-boiled eggs!

59.

Why do hens lay eggs?

If they dropped them, they'd break!

60.

What do you call an owl with a deep voice?

A growl!

61.
What is a polygon?

A parrot's that's flown away!

62.
How do chickens bake a cake?

From scratch!

63.
Why did the young bird get told off at school?

She was caught tweeting on a test!

64.

What do owls say when it rains heavily?

Too wet to woo!

65.

What might you call a clever duck?

A wise quacker!

66.

Why did the owl say, "Quack, quack, tweet, tweet"?

It didn't give a hoot!

67.

What game do parrots like to play?

Hide and Speak!

68.

What is an owl's favorite subject?

Owl-gebra!

69.

What do you get if you cross a duck with a firework?

A firequaker!

70.

What happened when the chicken decided to sleep under a car?

She woke oily the next morning!

71.

Why did the owl, 'owl?

Because the woodpecker would peck 'er!

72.

Where do penguins go to dance?

The snow ball!

73.

Which bird is always running out of breath?

A puffin!

74.

Where does a penguin keep its money?

In a snow bank!

75.

What is green and pecks on trees?

Woody Wood Pickle!

76.

What's a penguin's favorite part of a salad?

Iceberg lettuce!

77.

Who is a penguin's favorite aunt?

Aunt-Arctica!

78.

What do you call a bunch of chickens playing baseball?

Fowl play!

79.

Why do penguins catch fish in their beaks?

Because they can't hold fishing rods with their flippers!

80.

What do you call a woodpecker with no beak?

A headbanger!

81.

What is a penguin's favorite hat?

An ice cap!

82.
What kind of math do owls like?

Owlgebra!

83.
What is black and white, black and white, and black and white?

A penguin rolling down a hill!

84.
What is black, white and red all over?

A sunburnt penguin!

85.

What is the naughtiest bird?

A mockingbird!

86.

Why don't you see penguins in England?

Because they're afraid of Wales!

87.

What do penguins eat at restaurants?

Ice burg-ers!

88.

What did the goose say when she bought lipstick?

Put it on my bill!

89.

Why are penguins good racing drivers?

Because they're always in pole position!

90.

How do ducks drink?

Out of beak-ers!

91.

How do you help a sick bird?

Give it tweetment!

92.

Why did the chicken cross the road?

To get to the other side!

93.

Why did the chewing gum cross the road?

It was stuck to the chicken's foot!

94.

Why did the hen go halfway across the road and stop?

She wanted to lay it on the line!

95.

Why did the rooster not cross the road?

Because it was chicken!

96.

Why did the turkey cross the road?

It was the chicken's day off!

97.

Why did the turkey cross the road twice?

To prove it wasn't chicken!

98.

Why did the chicken cross the road, roll in mud, then cross the road again?

He was a dirty double crosser!

99.

What was the farmer doing on the other side of the road?

He was catching all the chickens!

100.

Why did the chicken cross the clothing store?

To get to the other size!

101.

Why did the chicken cross the playground?

To get to the other slide!

101 Fish Jokes for Kids

IP Factly Presents...

1.
Where do you get microwaves?

Tiny beaches!

2.
Why did the goldfish sell its old tank?

It couldn't work out how to drive it!

3.
How do prawns and clams communicate?

With shell-phones!

4.

Why is it easy to spot Cinderella-fish?

They have glass flippers!

5.

Why would an octopus vs. squid war be terrible?

Because they are both so well-armed!

6.

How do fish without cars get around?

Octo-bus!

7.
Why does the ocean twinkle at night?

It's full of starfish!

8.
Why are dolphins always innocent?

They never do anything on porpoise!

9.
What do you call a collection of very small oceans?

Sea-dlings!

10.

How does an ocean make itself taste good?

Sea-soning!

11.

How do shark dentists work?

Very carefully!

12.

Which sea creature does best at underwater math?

An octoplus!

13.

Why don't crabs share their food?

Because they're shellfish!

14.

What do giant squid like for dinner?

Fish and ships!

15.

How do you know the sea is glad to see you?

It waves!

16.

What do fish love to play?

Tide and seek!

17.

What's the fastest fish in the river?

A motor pike!

18.

Why do fish stay away from restaurants?

They are scared of getting battered!

19.

How does the sea like its hair?

Wavy!

20.

Why are fish the cleverest creatures in the sea?

They're always in schools!

21.

What do fish like playing at parties?

Bass the parcel!

22.

How do sealions send love letters?

Seal-ed with a kiss!

23.

How did the shellfish sail into college?

On a scallop-ship!

24.

What did the squid do when it left school?

Joined the army!

25.

What did the Pacific Ocean say to the Indian Ocean?

Nothing,they just waved!

26.

What did the Atlantic Ocean say to the Arctic Ocean?

Nothing, oceans can't speak!

27.

Which celebrity fish is always on TV?

The star-fish!

28.

Why are crabs never homeless?

There is always a seabed for them!

29.

Why are goldfish orange?

They got rusty!

30.

How did the goldfish become an old fish?

By taking away its G!

31.

Why don't mice swim in rivers?

They're scared of catfish!

32.

Why are fish so good for you?

They're full of vitamin Sea!

33.

Where do they make fish?

Finland!

34.

What fish do pirates use?

Swordfish!

35.

What happened to the man who crossed a wooden boy with a fish?

He made Fin-occhio!

36.

What kind of smart clothes do fish wear?

Fin striped suits!

37.
What is the most important fish at a hospital?

A sturgeon!

38.
What is the saddest creature in the ocean?

The blue whale!

39.
Which fish lives in a monastery?

A monkfish!

40.

What did the fish say when his friend sneezed?

Cod bless you!

41.

How do fish count the hours?

In fin-utes!

42.

What do South American fish use to read books?

An Amazon Fin-dle!

43.
Why did the lobster blush?

Because the sea weed!

44.
What do fish in the Colorado River say when they swim into a concrete wall?

Dam!

45.
Which fish are known for their miracles?

Angelfish!

46.

Where do fish go to wash and clean up?

A river basin!

47.

Which part of a fish gets into adventures with Tom Sawyer?

Huckleberry Fin!

48.

What fish make pianos sound nice?

Tunas!

49.

What are the strongest sea creatures?

Mussels!

50.

What's your best chance of catching fish?

Have the fishmonger throw them to you!

51.

Why are fish so bad at soccer?

They're scared of the net!

52.
What side of a fish has the most scales?

The outside!

53.
Why does the ocean not allow playgrounds?

It's afraid of sea-saws!

54.
Where's the best area for catching flatfish?

Anywhere - there's lots of plaices!

55.

Which fish swims best above the water?

A sailfish!

56.

How did the octopus get away with being rude?

He said he was just squidding!

57.

What do you get when you fling a white stone into the Black Sea?

A wet stone!

58.

What happens when you fling a white stone into the Red Sea?

It sinks!

59.

What's white and fluffy and lives underwater?

A sheep with a snorkel!

60.

Why did the fussy eater go fishing?

Just for the halibut!

61.

Who do fish always know their weight?

They have their own scales!

62.

What are the laziest creatures in the sea?

Slobsters!

63.

What do dolphins get from irritable sharks?

As far away as possible!

64.
What fish is always naked?

Bare-acudas!

65.
What seafood do restaurants at saunas offer?

Steamed mussels!

66.
What do fish love to watch on TV?

Whale of fortune!

67.

What did the shark say to its heartbroken friend?

Don't worry there's plenty more fish in the sea!

68.

Why did the sea roar?

It had crabs in its bed!

69.

How do dolphins and porpoises decide whose turn it is?

They flipper coin!

70.
Who won the underwater derby?

The sea-horse!

71.
Why did the crab cross the beach?

To get to the other tide!

72.
Where did the seaweed find a job in the paper?

In the kelp wanted section!

73.

What's the brightest fish in the sea?

A starfish

74.

Why do you rarely see a lionfish?

They can't hold the rods with their paws!

75.

Why don't sharks eat comedians?

They taste funny!

76.
Why do fish enjoy learning the piano?

They love their scales!

77.
What is a killer whale's favorite kind of music?

Orca-hestral!

78.
How did the octopus set up camp so quickly?

It was good with tent-acles!

79.

Why are seals so clever?

They train humans to stand and throw fish at them!

80.

Why was the rich octopus so careful?

In case it was squidnapped!

81.

What is the male child of an ocean called?

Sea-son!

82.

Where do fish keep their spare fins?

In a fin-cushion!

83.

What happened to the man who crossed a salmon and Nutella?

He got salmonella!

84.

How do squids in love walk along the sea floor?

Arm in arm in arm in arm in arm in arm...

85.

Why are crustaceans so irritable?

They are often crabby!

86

What do you call a man that keeps flatfish on his head?

Ray!

87.

What whale has the longest tongue in the animal kingdom?

Moby Lick!

88.
Which whale is ill all the time?

Moby Sick!

89.
What did one parrot say to the other parrot while sitting on a perch?

Can you smell fish?

90.
What did the seaweed shout when a fish began to eat it?

Kelp! Kelp!

91.

What is a fish's favorite time of year?

Fin-tertime!

92.

What is a fish's favorite sporting event?

The Fin-ter Olympics!

93.

Which fish can still get around when the water is frozen?

Skates!

94.

Why happened to the jellyfish that fell in a fridge?

It set!

95.

What happened to the man that put a big fish into the plug socket?

He got an electric shark!

96.

Where should you always weigh whales?

At the whale-weigh station!

97.

Where did Noah keep the fish with wheels?

In the carp-ark!

98.

When should you give your goldfish fresh water?

When they've finished what they've got!

99.

How can whales hear each other miles away?

They use herring aids!

100.

What did the fish magician say?

Pick a cod, any cod!

101.

What happened to the man who crossed a shark with a cow?

He was too scared to milk it!

101 Farmyard Jokes for Kids

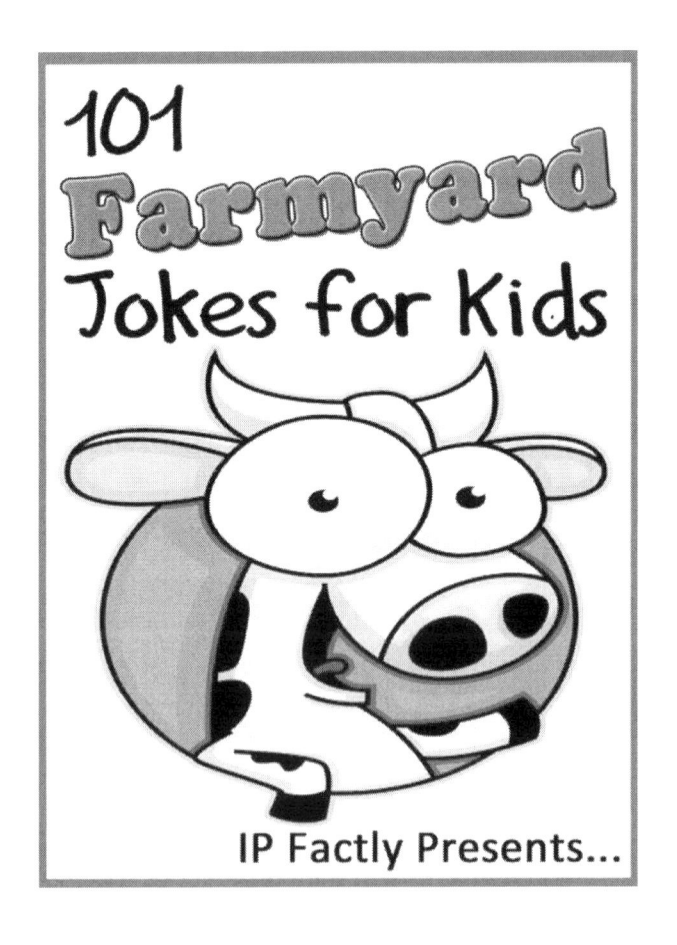

IP Factly Presents...

1.

What happened to the man who crossed a duck with a firework?

He got a firequacker!

2.

When doesn't a cockerel cock-a doodle-doo?

When it cock-a-doodle-don't!

3.

Where do pigs learn about magic?

Hogwarts School of Witchcraft and Wizardry!

4.

How did the pig leave the scene of the accident?

In a ham-bulance!

5.
How do cows disguise themselves?

With moo-staches!

6.
What do chicken scientists do?

Eggs-periments!

7.

When do ducks wake up?

At the quack of dawn!

8.

Why do sheep never leave the field?

They all stand at the gate saying, "After ewe!"

9.

Why was the cow always exercising?

It wanted to build up its moo-scles!

10.

What happened to the man who crossed chickens with a railway?

He invented eggs-press trains!

11.
Why did the sheep keep walking along the road?

It didn't see the ewe turn!

12.
Where do pigs live?

Hog cabins!

13.

Where did the young cows go on a school trip?

The moo-seum!

14.

What do you call polar cows?

Eski-moos!

15.

Why do horses look miserable all the time?

Because they walk around with long faces!

16.

When do hens wake up?

Seven o'cluck in the morning!

17.

What is a cow's favorite party game?

Moo-sical chairs!

18.

What happened to the man who fed his chickens gold?

He got eggs-pensive eggs!

19.

What happened to the man who crossed a cow with a goat?

He got a coat!

20.
What is the best-dressed horse?

A clotheshorse!

21.
Why are cows scared all the time?

They are cow-ards!

22.

What has 2 wings and says moo?

A cow in a plane!

23.

What happened to the man who crossed a cow with a drummer?

He got a moo-sician!

24.

What happened to the man who crossed sheep and hoops?

He discovered baa-sketball!

25.

Why do geese never go to restaurants?

They always get left with a big bill!

26.

What happened to the man who crossed a sheep with a kangaroo?

He got a woolly jumper!

27.

What do frogs and toads love to listen to?

Hip hop!

28.

What happened to the famous duck detective?

He quacked the case!

29.

What happens to rabbits after they get married?

They go on their bunny-moon!

30.

Where do toads leave their coats?

In the croakroom!

31.

How did the exited hen finish every sentence?

With an eggs-clamation point!

32.

What is a sheep's favorite animal at the zoo?

Baa-boon!

33.

What happened to the man who crossed a frog and a hare?

He got a ribbit!

34.

What do you call naughty pigs?

Grounded-hogs!

35.

Why don't rabbits like the book Watership Down?

They only like books with hoppy-endings!

36.

What happened to the man who crossed a cow and a chicken?

He got roost beef dinner!

37.
How do sheepdogs talk to sheep?

They baa-rk!

38.
When do cows call the first day of the year?

Moo Year's Day!

39.
Where did the lost cows of America go?

Nobody's herd!

40.

What happened to the man who crossed cows and toads?

He got bullfrogs!

41.

What type of sheep can jump higher than the moon?

All of them – the moon doesn't jump!

42.

How do you cure a coughing horse?

Cough stirrup!

43.

Who cut sheep's wool?

Baa-bers!

44.

What do cows like on their hot dogs?

Moo-stard!

45.

Why do the Amish ride horse and buggies into town?

Because they are too heavy to carry!

46.

How did the young boar wear her hair?

In pigtails!

47.

What did the farmer say to the hen boasting she would lay a million eggs?

Do not eggs-aggerate!

48.

What do cows like to eat for lunch?

Moo-shroom soup!

49.

What happened to the man who crossed an island of dinosaurs with some pigs?

Jurassic Pork!

50.

What happened to the man who crossed a cow and an earthquake?

He got a milkshake!

51.

Why don't cows listen to talk radio shows?

They prefer moo-sic!

52.

How do sheep sing?

Baa-dly!

53.

What do you call a male cow taking an afternoon nap?

A bulldozer!

54.

Why did the brown cow wear a bell?

Because its horns didn't work!

55.
Why don't pigs fly?

Because the price of ham would rise!

56.
What did the cow who barged the other cow say?

Moo-ve!

57.
How do farmers count their cows?

Cow-culators!

58.

What do horses play when not in the field?

Stable tennis!

59.

Why did the chicken, the turkey, the duck, and the goose all cross the road?

For some fowl reason!

60.

What happens to ponies that fall out of trees?

They go to the horse-pital!

61.

What happened to the man who crossed black and white animals with sheep?

He got baa-dgers!

62.

What did the mummy cow say to the baby cows stood next to a pile of poop?

Moo done it?

63.

Who steal pigs?

Hamburglars!

64.

What happened to the man who crossed a cow and an octopus?

He got an animal that milked itself!

65.

What did the lamb say when his mom gave him a present?

Thank ewe!

66.

What goes "moo -bang, moo – bang"?

Cows in a balloon factory!

67.

What happened to the man who crossed a cow with a cockerel?

He got an animal that mooed at the crack of dawn!

68.

What happened to the man who crossed a cow with a wolf?

He got an animal that mooed at the full moon!

69.

Where do hens get all their jokes?

Yolk books!

70.

Where do ducks save their money?

In a river bank!

71.

Why do bulls make so much noise?

They love using their horns!

72.

When doesn't a bull have horns?

When it's a bullfrog!

73.
What did the bus driver say to the toad?

Hop on!

74.
What kind of spring flower does a toad like best?

A croak-us!

75.
What do frogs drink?

Croak-a-cola!

76.

What kind pigs are always crashing their cars?

Road hogs!

77.

What is the world's best jumper?

A hiccupping frog!

78.

Why did the frog stop jumping?

It was un-hoppy!

79.
Which are the oldest rabbits?

The ones with gray hares!

80.
Why do cows like to do on a night out?

Go to watch moo-sicals!

81.
What do frogs buy at the candy store?

Lolli-hops!

82.

What do ducks do when their babies are ill?

Send them to the duck-tor!

83.

What do mice love to play?

Hide and squeak!

84.

What happened to the hen that ate some dynamite?

It eggs-ploded!

85.

How do sheep swim across rivers?

Baa-ckstroke!

86.

Why don't jockeys ride horses when the sun goes down?

They don't like night-mares!

87.

When did the rabbit go to the barbers?

When it was having a bad hare day!

88.

Why do farmers have to tell their cows jokes?

They need to be kept a*moo*sed!

89.

How do pigs hack trees down?

With pork chops!

90.

Why did the frog like it when its car broke down?

It enjoyed being toad for a change!

91.
Where do injured rabbits go?

The hopital!

92.
How do farmers fit thousands of pigs on their farm?

They build sty-scrapers!

93.
How do toads greet each other?

Wart's new with you!

94.

What happened to the man who crossed the Muppets with smog?

He got Kermit the Fog!

95.

What happened to the man who first crossed sheep and fire?

He invented baa-becues!

96.

What kind of cow eats the grass outside houses?

Lawn moo-ers!

97.

How did the frog say it was dying?

It croaked it!

98.

What happened to the man who crossed a horse and a cold?

He got hay fever!

99.

When did the horse answer the teacher's questions?

Whinney had to!

100.

What happened to the man who crossed Darth Vader and a frog?

He got Star Warts!

101.

Why do cows think they should group together in fields?

It's just what they herd!

101 School Jokes for Kids

IP Factly Presents...

1.

Why did the teacher get stronger bulbs for the school room?

Because the class was a little dim!

2.

Who's the king of your desk?

Your ruler!

3.

Why did the sun not bother going to college?

It already had a million degrees!

4.

History teacher: How did the Dark Ages get their name?

Pupil: From all the Knights!

5.

History teacher: How did Vikings communicate?

Pupil: Norse code!

6.

Headmaster: Why are your eyes crossed?

Teacher: I just can't control my pupils!

7.

History teacher: Why is England so wet?

Pupil: Because Kings and Queens have reigned there for centuries!

8.

Why did the music teacher get locked in his piano?

The keys were stuck on the outside!

9.

Teacher: Where might you find the English Channel?

Pupil: I don't know, is it near the MTV channel?

10.

What class does a butterfly like best?

Mothematics!

11.

Why do music teachers need stepladders?

To reach the high notes!

12.

Mother: How did you find school?

Son: It was there when I got off the bus!

13.

What's the worst thing ever found in a school cafeteria?

The Food!

14.

What kind of plates do Martians use at school?

Flying saucers!

15.

How can you guarantee straight A's?

Use a ruler!

16.

Why do noses hate going to school?

They are always getting picked on!

17.

Mother: How did you manage to get told off so many times today?

Son: I'm an early riser!

18.

History teacher: Who was the biggest knight at King Arthur's round table?

Pupil: Sir Cumference!

19.

Teacher: How do you get a higher education?

Pupil: Study on top of a mountain!

20.

Why are librarians good at fishing?

They've always got lots of bookworms to use as bait!

21.

Mother: How was your new teacher?

Son: Not good, she wanted to know how to spell cat!

22.

Why do librarians often talk about silent vegetables?

Because they are always saying "Quiet peas"!

23.

Why did the boy run into school 20 minutes late?

Because he had been told not to stroll into school 20 minutes late again!

24.

Where do music teachers go to find new pianos?

Florida Keys!

25.

Why did the teacher describe the boy's test results as underwater?

Because they were below 'C' level!

26.

Where do schools get their pens and pencils?

Pennsylvania!

27.

If I gave you fifty dollars and your father gave you another fifty what would you have?

A new bike!

28.

Headmaster: Why did you pass everything except history class?

Pupil: I didn't take history!

29.

Geography teacher: What is the capital of France?

Pupil: F!

30.

Math Teacher: If I lay one egg here, three over here and then two more here, how many eggs will there be?

Pupil: None! You can't lay eggs!

31.

History Teacher: What did William Tell's son say when the apple on his head was hit?

Pupil: That was an arrow escape!

32.

Geography teacher: Which country is known to be fast moving?

Pupil: Rusha!

33.

Teacher: How did Noah keep the ark illuminated?

Pupil: Floodlights!

34.

History Teacher: Why did Henry the eighth get through so many wives?

Pupil: He chopped and changed a lot!

35.

History Teacher: What would people have worn at the Boston Tea Party?

Party Hats!

36.

History teacher: What happened at the Boston Tea Party?

Annoyed pupil: I don't know - they didn't invite me!

37.
What's purple or green and can be seen from space?

The grape wall of China!

38.
History teacher: How did Romans greet their leaders when the weather was bad?

Pupil: Hail Caesar!

39.
Teacher: Who built the ark and saved the animals?

Pupil: I have No-ah idea!

40.

History teacher: Where was the Declaration of Independence signed?

Pupil: At the bottom!

41.

Teacher: What do Alexander the Great and Kermit the Frog have in common?

Pupil: Middle names!

42.

History teacher: Who cut the Roman Empire in half?

Pupil: A pair of Caesars!

43.

Geography teacher: Where are elephants found?

Pupil: In lost luggage!

44.

What kind of sum does a pupil like best?

Sum-mer!

45.

Teacher: Where is the best place to learn multiplication?

Pupil: On tables!

46.

Pupil: Why are you wearing sunglasses?

Teacher: Because you are all so bright!

47.

Teacher: Why did you miss school yesterday?

Pupil: I didn't, there's was plenty of things to do at home!

48.

Pupil: Why are you dipping your toes in the swimming pool Miss?

Teacher: I'm testing the water!

49.

Teacher: What would I have if I had 2 melons in this hand and 6 bananas in the other hand?

Pupil: Big hands!

50.

Teacher: What is the shortest month?

Pupil: May - with only three letters!

51.

Why do some teachers draw on windows?

To make the lesson clear!

52.

How do bees get to their lessons in a morning?

School buzz!

53.

What is special about the Mississippi river?

It has four eyes but can't see a thing!

54.

What is the name of the little rivers that flow into the Nile?

Juve-niles!

55.

Geography teacher: Where are the Andes?

Pupil: At the end of my sleevies!

56.

Why did Eve decide to go to New York?

She wanted a taste of the Big Apple!

57.

Geography teacher: Can you name the Poles?

Pupil: Yes, North, South and tad...!

58.

What meals do math teachers enjoy?

Square meals!

59.

Science teacher: How do we deal with crude oil?

Pupil: Send it to the headmaster!

60.

Teacher: How did Noah manage to design an ark?

Pupil: He was an ark-itect!

61.

History teacher: Where did the Pilgrims land when they got off the Mayflower?

Pupil: On the shore!

62.

History teacher: Where is Hadrian's Wall?

Pupil: Around his house!

63.

History teacher: Why does history repeat itself?

Pupil: Because no-one listens in history lessons!

64.

History teacher: Who came after the first President of the USA?

Pupil: The second President!

65.

Why did Noah never catch many fish?

He only had two worms!

66.

History Teacher: When was Rome built?

Pupil: At night - because Rome was not built in a day!

67.
Why are math books usually blue?

Because they have so many problems!

68.
History Teacher: What was King Arthur's Camelot?

Pupil: A place for the knights to park their camels!

69.
History Teacher: What was written on the headstones of knight's graves?

Pupil: Rust in peace!

70.

History teacher: Why did the dinosaurs go extinct?

Pupil: I don't know, that's more your era than mine!

71.

What famous commander invented fireplaces?

Alexander the grate!

72.

What happened when the horse walked into the classroom?

The teacher asked, "Why the long face?"!

73.

History Teacher: Why did Robin Hood rob the rich?

Pupil: The poor had nothing worth stealing!

74.

History teacher: Who invented fractions?

Pupil: Henry the 1/8th!

75.

History Teacher: Where did warriors in the middle ages learn to fight?

Pupil: At knight school!

76.

Geography teacher: What do you know about the Dead Sea?

Confused pupil: I didn't even know it was sick!

77.

History Teacher: When were the Pharaohs buried in pyramids?

Pupil: When they were dead!

78.

Geography teacher: What did Delaware…?

Pupil: A New Jersey!

79.

Pupil: What is your favorite rock group Miss?

Geography teacher: The Blue Ridge Mountains!

80.

Why are rabbits so good at math?

They are the quickest multipliers!

81.

Teacher: What would you have if you took home three dogs today and five tomorrow?

Pupil: A very angry mom!

82.

Teacher: What would you get if you add 342 and 286 and then multiply by 6?

Pupil: The wrong answer!

83.

What is a math teacher's favorite tree?

Geometr-ee!

84.

What kind of pliers might you need in a math lesson?

Multi-pliers!

85.

Teacher: Where are the Great Plains?

Pupil: In the airport!

86.

What would you have if you had an apple, an orange, a banana and five grapes?

A small fruit salad!

87.

Teacher: Who can include the word '*lettuce*' in a sentence?

Pupil: Can you *lettuce* go home now?

88.

Teacher: Who can include the word *'politics'* in a sentence?

Pupil: After the parrot ate my watch *Polly-tics*!

89.

Teacher: Who can include the word *'ambush'* in a sentence?

Pupil: I plucked some lovely ham from the *'am bush*!

90.

What is the best state to go to school?

Alabama - you are guaranteed four A's and one B!

91.

Math teacher: Do you need a pocket calculator?

Pupil: No, it's not pockets I'm struggling to count!

92.

Why was the library so tall?

It had lots of stories!

93.

Teacher: Who knows who broke the sound barrier?

Pupil: Johnny was playing with it last!

94.

Teacher: What's a mushroom?

Pupil: Another name for the school canteen!

95.

Why are school cooks so evil?

They beat eggs and whip cream!

96.

What is the first thing elves learn at school?

The elf-abet!

97.

Teacher: I hope I haven't just seen you copying from Johnny's test!

Pupil: I hope so too!

98.

Pupil: How did you know I copied from Johnny?

Teacher: For question 12 he wrote, "Don't know" and you wrote, "Me neither"!

99.

Teacher: What are you going to be when you leave school?

Pupil: Old!

100.

Mother: You got a terrible mark, why do you think your teacher likes you?

Son: All those kisses she wrote on my test!

101.

Teacher: Why are you doing cartwheels in my class?

Pupil: I'm turning things over in my mind!

101 Knock! Knock! Jokes for Kids

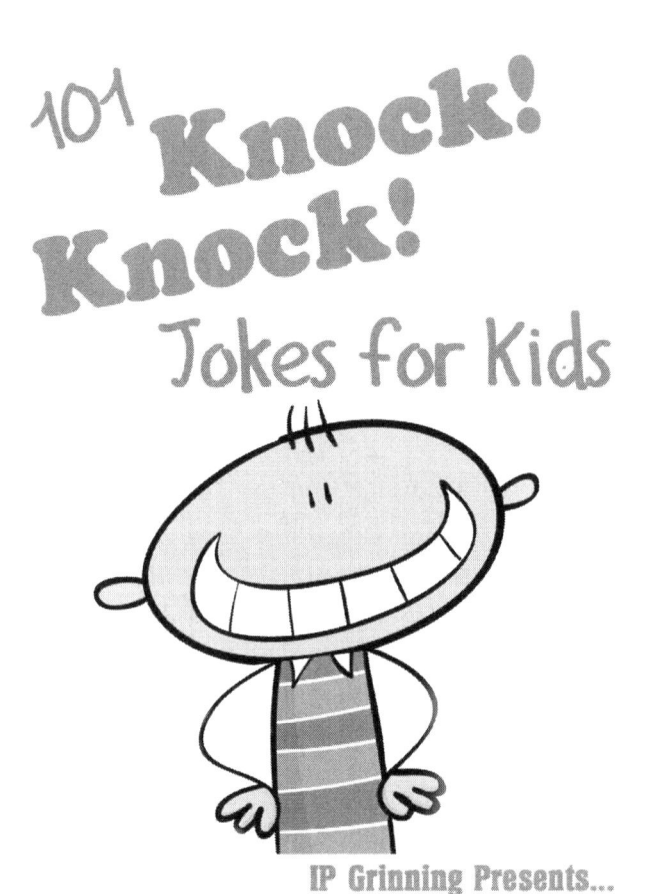

IP Grinning Presents...

1.
Knock Knock!

Who's there?

Randy.

Randy who?

Randy last three miles - I need a lie down!

2.
Knock Knock!

Who's there?

Letters.

Letters who?

Letters in and you'll find out!

3.

Knock Knock!

Who's there?

Turner.

Turner who?

Turner your music down!

4.

Knock Knock!

Who's there?

Ice cream.

Ice cream who?

Ice cream every time I see your face!

5.

Knock!

Who's there?

Eileen.

Eileen who?

Eileen down bang my head on your door and you ask "who's there?"

6.

Knock Knock!

Who's there?

Isabelle.

Isabelle who?

Isabelle not needed on your door?

7.

Knock Knock!

Who's there?

Underwear.

Underwear who?

I underwear the key is?

8.

Knock Knock!

Who's there?

Ben.

Ben who?

Ben wondering if you'd let me in?

9.

Knock Knock!

Who's there?

Ben.

Ben who?

Ben knocking on your door all morning!

10.

Knock Knock!

Who's there?

Doris.

Doris who?

Doris stuck – let me in!

11.

Knock Knock!

Who's there?

Anita.

Anita who?

Anita use the bathroom!

12.

Knock Knock!

Who's there?

Aida.

Aida who?

Aida pint of water and now I'm desperate!

13.
Knock Knock!

Who's there?

Lisa.

Lisa who?

Lisa you can do is let me use your bathroom!

14.
Knock Knock!

Who's there?

Butter.

Butter who?

Butter let me in, I'm desperate!

15.

Knock Knock!

Who's there?

Tank.

Tank who?

You're welcome!

16.

Knock Knock!

Who's there?

Isabelle.

Isabelle who?

Isabelle not working?

17.

Knock Knock!

Who's there?

Ali.

Ali who?

Ali tull old man who can't reach the doorbell!

18.

Knock Knock!

Who's there?

I could.

I could who?

I could reach the doorbell, but I shrank!

19.

Knock Knock!

Who's there?

Goose.

Goose who!

Goose who's knocking at your door?

20.

Knock Knock!

Who's there?

Luke.

Luke who?

Luke through the window and find out!

21.

Knock Knock!

Who's there?

Spider.

Spider who?

Spider through the keyhole!

22.

Knock Knock!

Who's there?

Wood.

Wood who?

Wood you let me in? It's freezing!

23.

Knock Knock!

Who's there?

Arch.

Arch who?

Bless You!

24.

Knock Knock!

Who's there?

Atish.

Atish who?

Are you catching a cold?

25.
Knock Knock!

Who's there?

Eddie.

Eddie who?

Eddie idea how to cure this cold!

26.
Knock Knock!

Who's there?

Hannah.

Hannah who?

Hannah me that screwdriver and I'll fix your doorbell!

27.

Knock Knock!

Who's there?

Colin.

Colin who?

Colin to see how you are!

28.

Knock Knock!

Who's there?

Cargo.

Cargo who?

No! Cargo "brum! brum!"

29.

Knock Knock!

Who's there?

Margo.

Margo who?

No! Margo "Tidy Your Room!"

30.

Knock Knock!

Who's there?

Cowgo.

Cowgo who?

No! Cowgo "Moo!"

31.

Knock Knock!

Who's there?

Moo.

Moo who?

Aah… Don't cry little cow!

32.

Knock Knock!

Who's there?

Soup.

Soup who?

Soup-erman!

33.
Knock Knock!

Who's there?

Olivia.

Olivia who?

Olivia, so get out my house!

34.
Knock Knock!

Who's there?

Water.

Water who?

Water you deaf or something?

35.

Knock Knock!

Who's there?

Lemonade.

Lemonade who?

Lemonade you in the purchase of a door-bell!

36.

Knock Knock!

Who's there?

Phillip.

Phillip who?

Phillip the gas tank, I'm almost out!

37.

Knock Knock!

Who's there?

Denis.

Denis who?

Denis says I need a tooth out!

38.

Knock Knock!

Who's there?

Bee.

Bee who?

Bee a dear and let me in!

39.
Knock Knock!

Who's there?

Ben.

Ben who?

Ben dover so I can kick you in the pants!

40.
Knock Knock!

Who's there?

Neil.

Neil who?

Neil down you're making me feel small!

41.

Knock Knock!

Who's there?

Watson.

Watson who?

What's on TV?

42.

Knock Knock

Who's there?

Cook.

Cook who?

Hey! Who are you calling cuckoo?

43.

Knock Knock!

Who's there?

Dishes.

Dishes who?

Dishes your friend, please let me in!

44.

Knock Knock!

Who's there?

Dishes.

Dishes who?

Dishes a nice doorstep, but let me in!

45.
Knock Knock!

Who's there?

Dishes.

Dishes who?

Dishes getting boring now! LET ME IN!

46.
Knock Knock!

Who's there?

Pickle.

Pickle who?

Pickle little flower for your momma!

47.

Knock Knock!

Who's there?

Jess.

Jess who?

Jess calling to see how you are!

48.

Knock Knock!

Who's there?

Les.

Les who?

Les go see a movie!

49.

Knock Knock!

Who's there?

Vaughan.

Vaughan who?

Vaughan day you'll buy a new doorbell!

50.

Knock Knock!

Who's there?

Annie.

Annie who?

Annie body calls, I'm on your doorstep!

51.

Knock Knock!

Who's there?

Annie.

Annie who?

Annie body going to let me in?

52.

Knock Knock!

Who's there?

Water.

Water who?

Water you doing? Just let me in!

53.

Knock Knock!

Who's there?

Safari.

Safari who?

Safari so good with the knock knock jokes!

54.

Knock Knock!

Who's there?

Aardvark.

Aardvark who?

Aardvark forward and open this door if I were you!

55.

Knock Knock!

Who's there?

Ivan.

Ivan who?

Ivan a new coat, do you like it?

56.

Knock Knock!

Who's there?

Ya.

Ya who?

What are you getting so excited about?

57.

Knock Knock!

Who's there?

Woo.

Woo who?

Stop getting so excited! They're only knock knock jokes!

58.

Knock Knock!

Who's there?

Wendy.

Wendy who?

Wendy going to let me in?

59.

Knock Knock!

Who's there?

Justin.

Justin who?

Justin time for lunch!

60.

Knock Knock!

Who's there?

Lee.

Lee who?

Lee me alone I'm tired!

61.

Knock Knock!

Who's there?

Police.

Police who?

Police help me stop telling knock knock jokes!

62.

Knock Knock!

Who's there?

Bet.

Bet who?

Bet you don't know who's at the door!

63.

Knock Knock!

Who's there?

Hugh.

Hugh who?

Hugh won't believe your eyes!

64.

Knock Knock!

Who's there?

Sabina.

Sabina who?

Sabina long time since I've seen you!

65.

Knock Knock!

Who's there?

Lass.

Lass who?

Lass time I saw you was 2 years ago!

66.

Knock Knock!

Who's there?

Pierre.

Pierre who?

Pierre through the keyhole to see me!

67.

Knock Knock!

Who's there?

Sam.

Sam who?

Sam day you'll remember me!

68.

Knock Knock!

Who's there?

Dwayne.

Dwayne who?

Dwayne the bathtub, I'm dwowning!

69.

Knock Knock!

Who's there?

Nana.

Nana who?

Nana your business!

70.

Knock Knock!

Who's there?

Waiter.

Waiter who?

Waiter right there, I've got more doors to knock on!

71.

Knock Knock!

Who's there?

Zany.

Zany who?

Zany body in?

72.

Knock Knock!

Who's there?

Ida.

Ida who?

Ida epic journey getting here!

73.

Knock Knock!

Who's there?

Comb.

Comb who?

Comb on open the door!

74.

Knock Knock!

Who's there?

Despair.

Despair who?

Despair tire was flat, can I use your phone?

75.

Knock Knock!

Who's there?

Nobel.

Nobel who?

Nobel, that's why I knocked!

76.

Knock Knock!

Who's there?

Unite.

Unite who?

Unite a person, and then you call him Sir!

77.

Knock Knock!

Who's there?

Howl.

Howl who?

Howl you know unless you open the door!

78.

Knock Knock!

Who's there?

Scott.

Scott who?

Scott nothing to do with you!

79.

Knock Knock!

Who's there?

Disguise.

Disguise who?

Disguise after me! Let me in!

80.

Knock Knock!

Who's there?

Ken.

Ken who?

Ken I come in, it's raining?

81.

Knock Knock!

Who's there?

Formosa.

Formosa who?

Formosa the summer I was on holiday!

82.

Knock Knock!

Who's there?

Island.

Island who?

Island on your roof with my parachute!

83.

Knock Knock!

Who's there?

Dakota.

Dakota who?

Dakota has no hood and it's raining!

84.

Knock Knock!

Who's there?

Radio.

Radio who?

Radio not, here I come!

85.

Knock Knock!

Who's there?

Juno.

Juno who?

Juno your door is locked!

86.

Knock Knock!

Who's there?

Seymour.

Seymour who?

Seymour if you open the door!

87.

Knock Knock!

Who's there?

Viper.

Viper who?

Viper your nose - it's running!

88.

Knock Knock!

Who's there?

Howie.

Howie, who?

Howie bout opening the door!

89.
Knock Knock!

Who's there?

Owl.

Owl who?

Owl be sad if you don't let me in!

90.
Knock Knock!

Who's there?

Baby owl.

Baby owl who?

Baby owl see you later, maybe I won't!

91.

Knock Knock!

Who's there?

Twitter.

Twitter who?

It's that baby owl again!

92.

Knock Knock!

Who's there?

Who.

Who who?

Will all the owls please leave -NOW!

93.

Knock Knock!

Who's there?

Ammonia.

Ammonia who?

Ammonia going to ask you once!

94.

Knock Knock!

Who's there?

Henrietta.

Henrietta who?

Henry –ate-a worm in an apple!

95.

Knock Knock!

Who's there?

Betty.

Betty who?

Betty wishes he had a coat like this!

96.

Knock Knock!

Who's there?

Imogen.

Imogen who?

Imogen life with a doorbell!

97.

Knock Knock!

Who's there?

Finders.

Finders who?

Finders my keys, I can't get in!

98.

Knock Knock!

Who's there?

Chicken.

Chicken who?

Chicken your pockets - I think you might have my keys!

99.

Knock Knock!

Who's there?

Donut!

Donut who?

Donut look now but there's a lion behind you!

100.

Knock Knock!

Who's there?

Lionel.

Lionel who?

Lionel eat you if you come in!

101.

Knock Knock!

Who's there?

Candice.

Candice who?

Candice be the last Knock Knock joke please?

Thank you for reading!

Thank you so much for buying this book. I hope you've enjoyed reading it as much as I enjoyed writing it.

To read more books search for
IP Grinning at Amazon.com

Printed in Great Britain
by Amazon